Life is Weird

(and other Noble Truths)

Laurie Fisher Huck

ELEMENT
CHILDREN'S BOOKS

SHAFTESBURY, DORSET · BOSTON, MASSACHUSETTS · MELBOURNE, VICTORIA

First published in the UK in 1998 by
Element Children's Books, Shaftesbury, Dorset SP7 8BP

Published in Australia in 1998 by Element Books Ltd for
Penguin Books Australia Ltd, 487 Maroondah Highway,
Ringwood, Victoria 3134

First published in 1997 by Weatherhill, Inc, of New York
and Tokyo, 568 Broadway, Suite 705, New York, NY10012

British Library Cataloguing in Publication data available

ISBN 1 901881 14 8

Cover design by Ness Wood
Printed in Hong Kong through Worldprint

To my
Mom and Dad

SUFFERING

First,

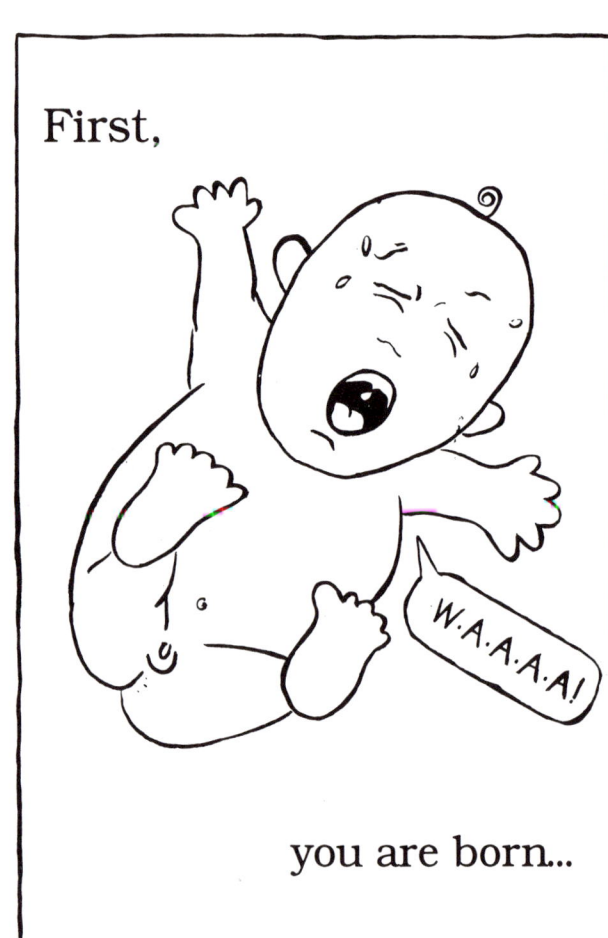

you are born...

...into
a tiny, helpless body
with stomach gas,
colic,
butt rash,
and *zero* bladder control.

And then,
you start growing old.

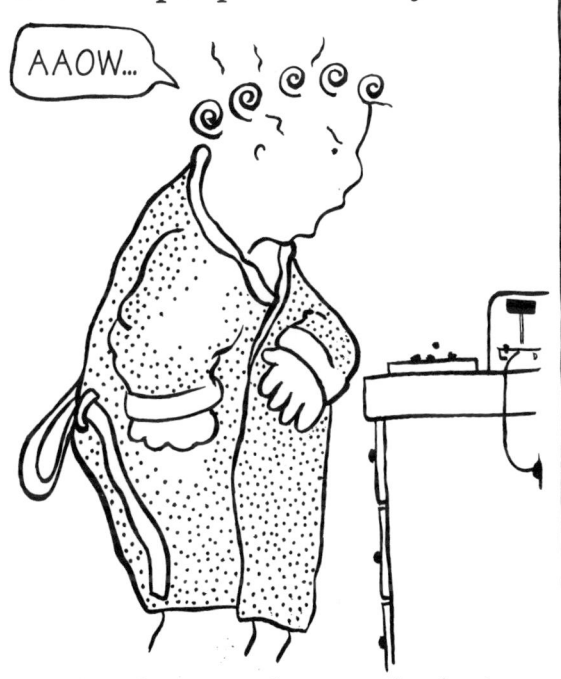

And things you have

that you don't want.

And there are plenty of opportunities to feel:

bored,
irritated,
jealous,
grossed-out,
afraid,
angry,
sad,
lonely,
inadequate,
threatened,
chubby,
stupid,
unappreciated,
unloved,
ugly,
unsuccessful,
squirrely,
and
totally bummed.

So...

Maybe you...

leave home,
fall in love,
get a "good" job,
buy a house,
> *a car,*
> *a swimming pool,*
> *a home entertainment unit,*
> *two huskies,*
> *a cottage,*
> *a boat,*
> *another car,*
> *a jacuzzi,*
> *an acquarium,*
> *a golf cart...*

...but still you feel hassled, so you...

take a luxury holiday,
join an athletic club,
go to more downtown restaurants,
"get into" art,
invest in the stockmarket,
have a child,
add on to your house,
redecorate,
refinance,
get a "better" job...

...but still you're not *happy* happy
like you think you should be,
soooo.... you...

fall out of love,
enter therapy,
take a shamanic journey,
give up meat,
join a food co-op,
move to the country,
buy a house,
redecorate,
find your inner child,
meet your soul-mate,
become an eco-activist,
quit your job,
reinvest your portfolio,
see a psychic,
have another child,
become a real estate agent,
get into crystals,
visit the Amazon...

...and you think maybe you're
happier...but still...
there's something...
surely you deserve _more_?

But the *whole world* is
so full of hassles... there's...

chemical warfare,
widespread poverty,
corruption,
exploitation,
political chaos,
social unrest,
discrimination,
waste,
slaughter,
pollution,
homeless children...

...you really should *do*
something about it all but...

the lawn needs mowing,
your son is "special,"
your accountant "must talk,"
the dog has distemper,
you're getting fat,
there's a funny lump,
your new boss is strange,
you're nervous, fidgety, short-
tempered, eating out of control...

...and just
when you feel
your time
has finally come
to stand up
and
really
make a difference
in this world...

Hassles,

suffering,

disappointment,

these are all a part of life...

...and then you die.

Weird.

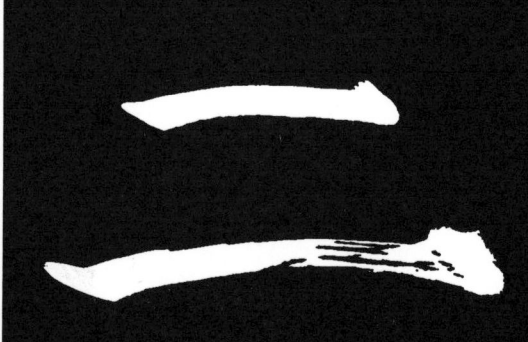

ORIGIN OF
SUFFERING

Some things
you just can't help.
If you have a body,
it's going to
grow old
and die.

No way around that.

Instead of just stopping
and trying to understand
what life is *really* about,
we just keep grabbing
at stuff we think will make
us happy, or cool, or sexy,
or powerful, or secure.

And the more we grab,
the more trouble we
cause ourselves...
and the more trouble
we cause our world.

If you could be
completely honest
with yourself,
you'd admit you only have it
so girls will think you're sporty.

And they do...for a minute...
until they realize your legs
are so short you can't run.
Then you feel even worse.

Truth is:

Nothing
we grab on to
will make us
"happy-ever-after".

Not a frog prince.
(He'll croak.)

Not the big important job.
(Stars fall.)

Not the best of anything.
(Wait 'til you see next year's model.)

Things change.
You can count on that.

They're impermanent.

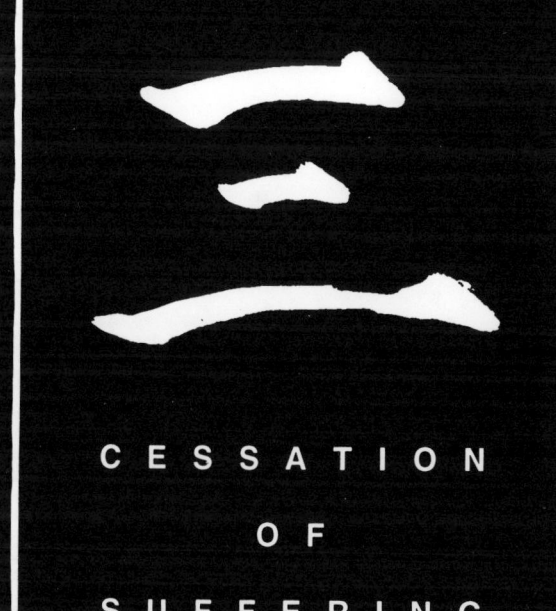

CESSATION

OF

SUFFERING

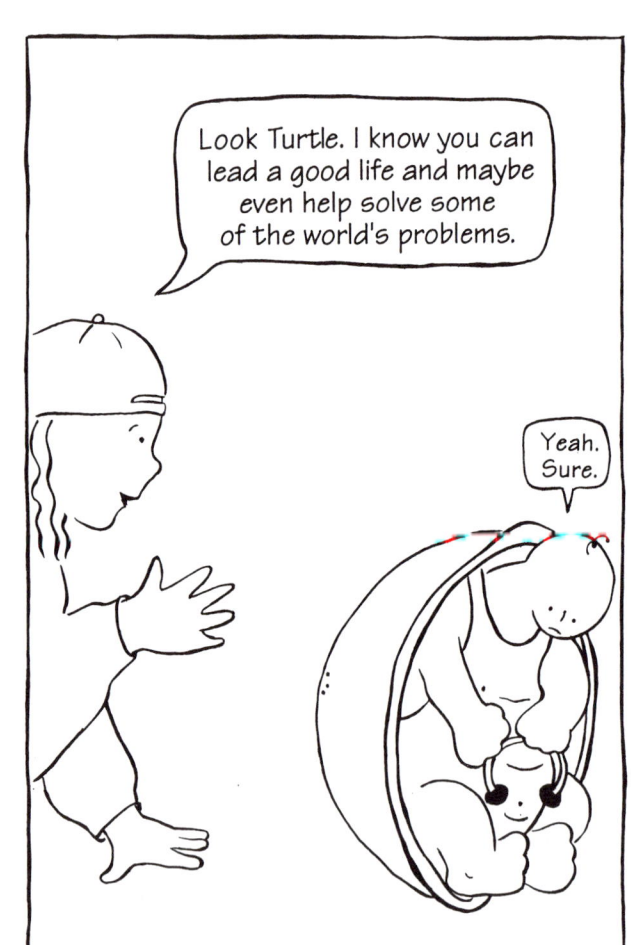

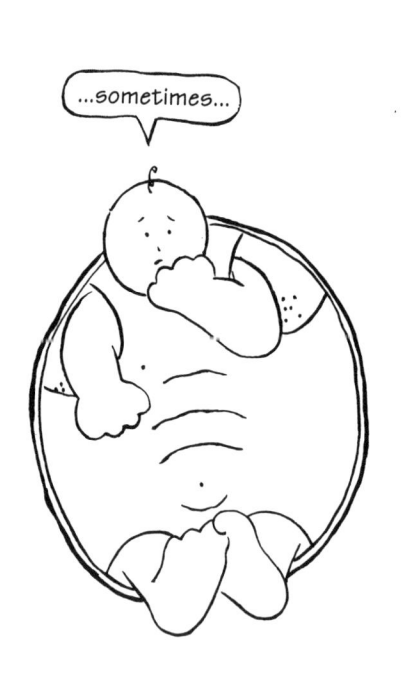

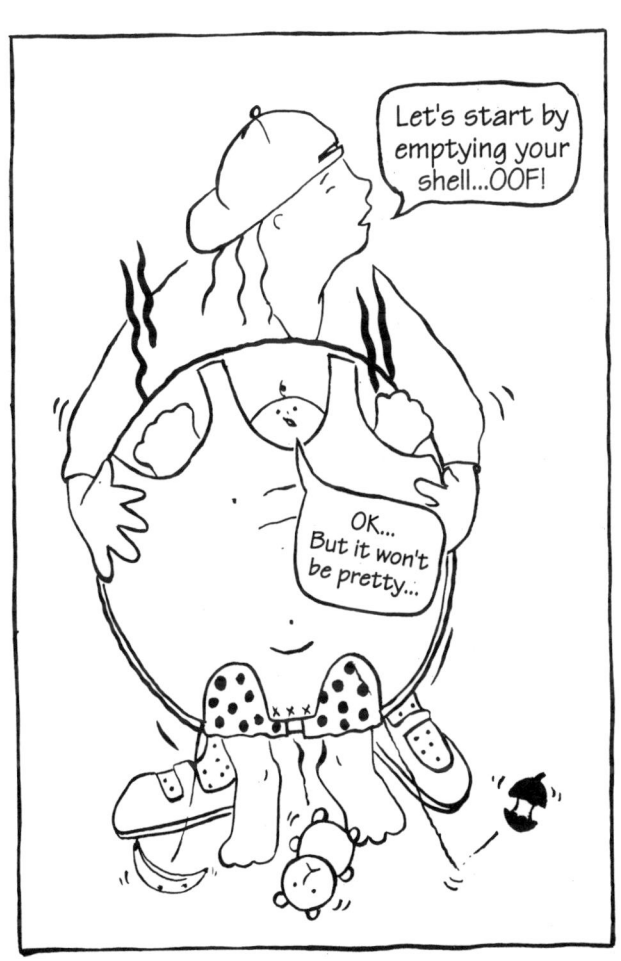

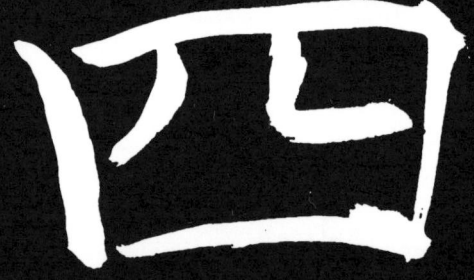

THE PATH

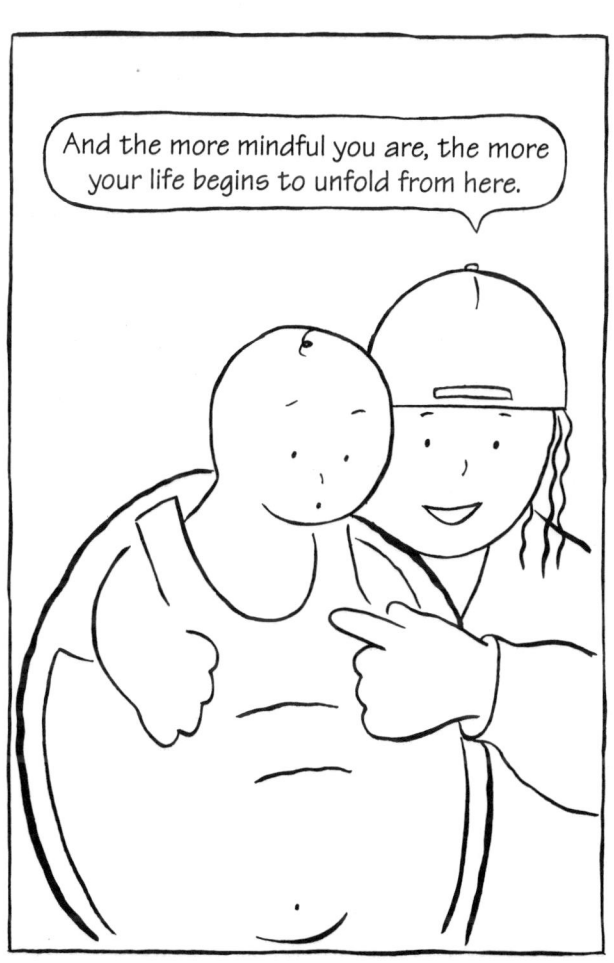

A Note from the Author

I didn't make up The Four Noble Truths. The Buddha taught them 2500 years ago. As you can see, they still work pretty well today.

We *all* get confused and we *all* experience suffering. Being confused doesn't mean you're bad. It means you need to come back to who you really are...to where your heart is. Meditation is an excellent way to come back. It doesn't fix things, but it can help you understand what this life is about...simply, clearly, directly.

Laurie Fisha Huck

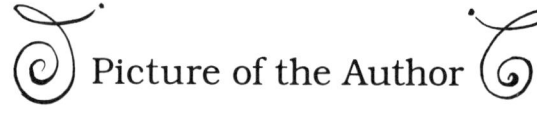

Picture of the Author

...in turtle-mode.